HOW & WHY TO:

PRAY FOR HEALING, PRAY IN TONGUES & GIVE PROPHECY

JENNIFER N. BUCZYNSKI

HOW & WHY TO: PRAY FOR HEALING, PRAY IN TONGUES & GIVE PROPHECY
Published by Jennifer N. Buczynski
www.growinginJesus.com

Copyright ©2011 Jennifer N. Buczynski
All rights reserved. Except for brief excerpts for review purposes,
no part of this book may be reproduced or used in any form
without prior written permission from the publisher.

Unless otherwise identified, all Scripture quotations are taken from the
New American Standard Bible®. Copyright ©1960, 1962, 1963, 1968, 1971,
1972, 1973, 1975, 1977, 1995 by The Lockman Foundation. Used by permission.

Scripture quotations marked (AMP) are taken from the Amplified Bible,
Copyright ©1954, 1958, 1962, 1964, 1965, 1987 by The Lockman Foundation.
Used by permission.

Scriptures marked (KJV) are taken from The Holy Bible,
Authorized King James Version ©1961 by The National Publishing Co.

Scripture quotations marked (NLT) are taken from the Holy Bible,
New Living Translation. Copyright ©1996, 2004, 2007. Used by permission
of Tyndale House Publishers Inc., Carol Stream, Illinois 60188. All rights reserved.

Scripture quotations marked (RSV) are taken from the Revised Standard Version
of the Bible, copyright ©1946, 1952, and 1971 National Council of the Churches
of Christ in the United States of America. Used by permission. All rights reserved.

ISBN-13: 978-0615548241 (pbk.)
ISBN-10: 0615548245 (pbk.)

Book design by Jamie Lynn Bell // www.FreeChurchWebsites.com

"Follow You into the World" and "Complete in Him" typefaces
created by Kimberly Geshwein // www.kimberlygeshwein.com
Used by permission.

Printed in the United States of America
First Edition 2011

THIS BOOK IS DEDICATED TO:

The Church of Jesus Christ around the globe.
May you again turn the world around as you are filled and refilled with the power of the Holy Spirit!

TABLE OF CONTENTS

INTRODUCTION iii
CH. 1: HOW & WHY TO PRAY FOR HEALING 1
CH. 2: HOW & WHY TO PRAY IN TONGUES 15
CH. 3: HOW & WHY TO GIVE PROPHECY 29
CONCLUSION 61
ACKNOWLEDGMENTS 67

INTRO:

Hi! Because you have picked up this book today, I can safely assume that in one way or another, you are interested in spiritual gifts from God the Holy Spirit.

Generally speaking, I can also assume that you have one of these four opinions:

- You believe spiritual gifts and miracles no longer exist today
- You believe spiritual gifts and miracles never existed
- You don't know much about spiritual gifts, but you would like to hear more about them

OR

- You are a big fan of spiritual gifts and you're just interested in what I have to say

If you can identify with one of the first three options, you are in good company! I was once where you are now. It was a matter of months and a big change of heart that brought me into the fourth group—but let me stop there for now!

Here's a bit more about me: the author. You obviously know my name (if you don't, just look at the cover!), and that I am a follower of Jesus Christ. I grew up in Buffalo NY, with three younger brothers and both of my parents. I generally heard very little about the spiritual gifts that God gives His children, so I mostly avoided the topic. But there came a cold November day during college, when God brought it all to my attention. I came face-to-face with God's supernatural power & gifts. My first reactions were of fear and disbelief. Here are a few pages from my prayer journal that I wrote as I studied the book of Acts to discover what all the hype was about!

11-20-06   49

Wow

"You shall receive _power_ when the Holy Spirit has come upon you, and you shall be witnesses in Jerusalem and Judea and Samaria and to the end of the earth" (Acts 1:8 RSV, Christ's words!)

"sound came from heaven like the rush of a mighty wind, and it _filled_ _all_ _the_ _house_ where they were sitting. And there appeared to them tongues as of a fire, distributed and resting on _each_ _one_ of them.

And they were all filled with the Holy Spirit and began to speak in other tongues, as the Spirit gave them utterance."
(Acts 2:2-4 RSV)

"...at this sound the multitude came together, and they were BEWILDERED because each one heard them speaking in his own language and they were AMAZED and WONDERED" (asking how that could be)!
(Acts 2:6-7 RSV)

(Acts 2:12 RSV)
"And all were amazed and perplexed, saying to one another:

'What does this MEAN?!' But others mocking said, 'They are filled w/ new wine.'"
(Acts 2:12-13 RSV)

    I feel like a mocker... like, "if I can't understand or explain this, it must not be real."

"I will pour out my Spirit upon all flesh, and your sons and your daughters shall prophesy...
I will pour out my spirit and they shall prophesy."
(Acts 2:17, 18 RSV)

"Now when they heard this (the Gospel) they were cut to the heart, and said to Peter and the apostles,

'Brethren, what shall we do?'

v

And Peter said to them, "Repent, and BE BAPTIZED every one of You in the name of Jesus Christ for the forgiveness of your sins; and you shall receive the gift of the Holy Spirit." (Acts 2:37-38 RSV)

"And FEAR came upon every soul; and many wonders and signs were done through the apostles." (Acts 2:43 RSV)

I'm not the only one who fears!!

"And when they had prayed, the place in which they were gathered together was shaken; and they were all filled with the Holy Spirit and spoke the Word of God with BOLDNESS." (Acts 4:31 RSV)

- Keith said tonight,
"the book of Acts is coming true! It's happening right now!"

Now I know what he meant.

As you can see, I longed to know God more; I longed to know the truth. I also recognized the fear I felt. I was very afraid. But I pressed on, because I knew that God did not give me a spirit of fear (see 2 Timothy 1:7). God soon reminded me, as I wrote in my journal the next day, one of the most frequent phrases in the Bible is one that the angels are always saying: "Do not fear."

No matter how confused you are, remember to listen to His word, and to follow His command: do not be afraid. Instead, trust God and pray that He will lead you to the right conclusions by studying His Word and listening to His Spirit (more on that later!)

As I continued to study and learn what God's Word had to say, I eventually came to this conclusion:

What is God if He is not utterly supernatural? He is greater than nature, and surely He is able to bend natural law.

Some (maybe even you!) have believed that God stopped giving out spiritual gifts and doing miracles after the Bible was finalized, because then the Gospel could be read. But the Good News is not just words on a page, it is the power of the Holy Spirit working in and through God's children who have been washed clean in the blood of Jesus. The Apostle Paul wrote that he would not preach the Gospel without signs and wonders because that would be an incomplete Gospel (Romans 15:18-19). If you study the biblical book of Acts, like I was driven to do, or if you read Christian history books, you will find miracles, healing, prophecy and other supernatural events throughout time.

God has always been a God of supernatural power: there were miracles in the Old and the New Testament. Jesus Christ is the same yesterday, today, and forever (Hebrews 13:8).

So before you read on, why don't you ask God for more faith?

Prophecy, tongues, healing and all the gifts of the Holy Spirit are given to us to build up the church and to further God's Kingdom on the earth before Jesus' second coming.

HOW & WHY TO PRAY FOR HEALING

I've heard a lot about healing recently. Does God really do that stuff?

I'm glad to see you've got some questions about healing! Healing is such a beautiful work of God—and it's so exciting!

First of all, I want to discuss healing in a biblical context. In the New and Old Testaments, healing was one of the most common ways that God blessed believers and brought unbelievers to Him. God healed through the prayers of His people, and also through the actions of those who represented Him on the earth.

Let's look together at some Old Testament examples of healing. Be prepared for lots of Scripture!

Okay, if you say so!

In the Old Testament—**(Exodus 15:26)**—God proclaimed that He was Israel's "healer.[1]" Kings like Hezekiah[2] and Jereboam[3] asked God's prophets to pray that God would heal them, and He did. The authors of the Psalms also pleaded for God to heal them,[4] and Moses prayed for his sister's healing.[5] The Lord declares that He will heal His people.[6] **Psalm 103:2-3** says, "Bless the Lord, O my soul, and forget none of His benefits; who pardons all your iniquities, who heals all your diseases." Healing was a part of God's character in the Old Testament.

Okay, so God healed in the Old Testament. But Jesus changed some things when He came, right? What was Jesus' take on healing?

If you've ever read the New Testament, you know that Jesus Himself healed multitudes of diseases and illnesses. In each Gospel, Jesus healed. In Matthew, when John the Baptist asked Jesus if He was the Messiah, Jesus responded by saying that the blind, deaf and lame were being healed and the Gospel was being preached to the poor.[7] These healings and His preaching were proof enough for John. Jesus healed lepers,[8,9] a sick woman,[10] sick children,[11] paralyzed people[12] and Peter's mother-in-law who had a fever.[13] He straightened a woman's disfigured

---

1	Exodus 15:26
2	2 Kings 20:8
3	1 Kings 13:6
4	Psalm 6:2, 41:4
5	Numbers 12:13
6	Isaiah 57:18
7	Matthew 11:2-5
8	Matthew 11:2-5
9	Luke 5:13
10	Mark 5:25-29
11	Matthew 15:28
12	Matthew 8:5-14
13	Matthew 8:5

back,[14] cured an invalid,[15] and when provoked by the Pharisees, Jesus healed a man's withered hand![16] On the night of His arrest, Jesus even reattached an ear that was sliced off by a sword![17] During His ministry on earth, people quickly learned of Jesus' healing power, and they brought crowds of sick people to Him to be cured. This was recorded in various places, including **Matthew 14:35-36** and **Mark 6:56**. **Luke 4:40** says, "All those who had any who were sick with various diseases brought them to Him; and laying His hands on each one of them, He was healing them."

So it's obvious that Jesus healed. But He's God! Of course He could do that. But what does that mean for everyday people like me?

If you want to hear about normal people who prayed for healing, just study the disciples and apostles. Many of these men were "unlearned"—they had no formal education. After Peter and John healed a man at Gate Beautiful, the government "perceived that they were uneducated, common men, [and] they were astonished. And they recognized that they had been with Jesus" **(Acts 4:13)**. In the book of Acts alone, there are at least nine different accounts of individual or group healings administered by the disciples.[18]

So the apostles and disciples healed too? It wasn't just Jesus?

That's right! While Jesus had His own visible ministry on earth, He was also training His disciples to be just like Him. **Luke 10** and **Matthew 10** both record Jesus instructing His disciples in the same methods of healing. "Jesus summoned His twelve disciples and gave

---

14	Luke 13:11-12
15	John 5:3-9
16	Matthew 12:10-13
17	Luke 22:51
18	Acts 3:6-8; 5:16; 8:7; 9:18; 9:34; 14:9-10; 19:12; 28:8,9

them authority over unclean spirits, to cast them out, and to heal every kind of disease" **(Matthew 10:1)**. Jesus actually told the disciples to "Heal the sick, raise the dead, cleanse the lepers, cast out demons. Freely you received, freely give" **(Matthew 10:8)**. Jesus gave the disciples the authority to heal and told them to do so.

I'm surprised.
So praying for healing was like a responsibility for the disciples?

Yes, it was a command from the Lord!

After Jesus went to heaven, did the disciples still obey Jesus' command to heal?

When the Lord Jesus was healing on earth, He got a lot of attention. As I mentioned earlier, sick people were brought to Jesus to be healed. Due to His reputation, Jesus captured the crowd's attention. The attention He received enabled Him to teach them about the Kingdom of God, repentance and forgiveness. The disciples must have seen this, because healing and other signs and wonders are all over the pages of the book of Acts. Just like Jesus modeled, when people were healed, the apostles took advantage of the crowds and taught about Jesus' death and resurrection, the importance of repentance and turning from sin to receive His salvation. After Pentecost, the Church prayed this prayer, as recorded in the book of Acts: "And now, Lord, take note of their threats, and grant that Your bond-servants may speak Your word with all confidence, while You extend Your hand to heal" **(Acts 4:29-30)**.

So, the answer to your question is yes!

Now I'm interested! Do we have any examples of the early Church and healing? How did they do it?

Now those are two questions with different answers! Where to begin! Okay, let's start with the first healing after Jesus ascended to heaven. In the third chapter of Acts, two of the disciples went to the temple. Outside the temple was a man that sat and begged for money every day. Everyone knew him because he was lame—he couldn't walk, and he always had to be carried. The man saw Peter and John and asked them for money.

> "But Peter said, 'I do not possess silver and gold, but what I do have I give to you: In the name of Jesus Christ the Nazarene—walk!'" **(Acts 3:6)**

The Bible tells us that when he said this, Peter "raised him up; and immediately his feet and his ankles were strengthened. With a leap he stood upright and began to walk; and he entered the temple with them, walking and leaping and praising God" **(Acts 3:7-8)**. As a result, 2,000 more people were saved **(see Acts 4:4)**. All Peter did was command this guy to walk and help him stand and BAM! He was healed!

Another healed individual was a man named Aeneas in **Acts 9**. He had been bedridden for eight years. When Paul saw him, he simply said: "Aeneas, Jesus Christ heals you; get up and make your bed" **(Acts 9:34)**. He just spoke and it happened! Once again, people were saved as a result—all who were present believed. Also in **Acts 5:44** and **8:7**, the disciples prayed and multitudes of sick people were healed.

There are even amazing stories of people being healed because they were in Peter's shadow **(Acts 5:15)**. And **Acts 19:11-12** explains that people were even healed just by touching a handkerchief or an apron that Paul had worn! Now how's that for extraordinary?!

Wow! That's intense. I guess Paul and Peter must have been pretty holy men. The methods they used for healing are really different. Did Jesus heal in the same ways?

There are no biblical records of Jesus healing with handkerchiefs or shadows, but He sure did heal in plenty of other ways. There are a lot of cool accounts of what Jesus did to heal people.

BLINDNESS:

- **Matt 9:27-29** | Jesus touched their eyes.
- **Mark 8:22-25** | Jesus took him out of the village, spit on his eyes and laid hands on him. Jesus had to pray for this man twice!
- **John 9:1-7** | Jesus mixed His spit with mud, put it on the man's eyes and told him to wash in the Pool of Siloam. The man obeyed and was healed!

DEAFNESS:

- **Mark 7:32-35** | Jesus took him away from the crowd, put His fingers in the man's ears, He spit, touched the man's tongue and told the ears to be opened!

LAME/PARALYZED:

- **John 5:3-9** | Jesus ordered him to stand and walk.

LEPERS:

- **Matthew 8:2-3** | The man said to Jesus, "Lord, if You are willing, You can make me clean." Jesus said, "I am willing; be cleansed."

VARIOUS SICKNESS:

- **Matthew 9:20-22** | A woman touched Jesus' garment in hopes of being healed. Jesus said that it was her faith that made her well.
- **Matthew 8:14-15** | Peter's mother-in-law had a fever and Jesus touched her.

That's amazing! He had so many different ways for healing the sick. I bet that's why the disciples had so many methods too.

You're probably right. But in addition to trying to be like Jesus, they probably had many different methods because they listened to the Holy Spirit. Even when two people have the same physical illness, God may heal them in completely different ways—just look at the list of blind men who were healed. For some, Jesus touched their eyes; for others, He used his spit.

Yikes. I'm glad Jesus doesn't have to spit on my eyes! Blech!

You're telling me! Anyway, in addition to these examples we have, God also gave us, the Church, some guidelines for healing. You're about to hear some more reasons (and ways) to pray for healing!

As the Church of Jesus Christ, we have to work together. You've already read how important healing was in the early Church—it paved a way for the message of Jesus and ultimately brought about salvation. Jesus taught His disciples about healing and they healed in a variety of ways.

The gift of healing is mentioned in the list of spiritual gifts in
1 Corinthians 12.

> "But to each one is given the manifestation of the Spirit for the common good. For to one is given…faith by the same Spirit, and to another gifts of healing by the one Spirit…But one and the same Spirit works all these things, distributing to each one individually as He wills." **(1 Corinthians 12:7, 8a, 9,11)**

Wait, wait. Healing is a GIFT? I thought it was a command! So everyone can't pray for healing?

Admittedly, this is a little bit confusing. Healing is a spiritual gift, as we see here. But praying for healing is also a command for all believers. **1 Corinthians 12:30** says, "All do not have gifts of healings, do they? All do not speak with tongues, do they?" It is true that every believer does not have the same spiritual gifts. It seems that some are more gifted with the ability to heal in Jesus' Name.

That reminds me. Sometimes I hear other believers accusing "healers" of being false Christians. What do you have to say about that?

Some Christians are in the public arena more than others. As a result of mistakes made in front of others, they are likely to be chastised harshly. Unfortunately, this judgmental attitude in the Church likely stems from some well known Christians in the past who practiced the gift of healing, but committed serious sin near the end of their ministries and fell away from God. These historical figures have caused a lot of doubt in the gift of healing today.

I think that some believers are gifted with the ability to heal more than other Christians. It is entirely possible, and entirely biblical, in my opinion, mainly because of these verses I just told you about.

"...to another, gifts of healing by the one Spirit," and "all do not have gifts of healings, do they?" **(1 Corinthians 12:9, 30)**.

But usually what bothers people is not the idea that some pray for healing and see results more frequently than others, the problem comes when they see visibly gifted Christians committing various kinds of sin in the public eye. This is a real problem, as with any Christian in leadership, and it exists not only in those who pray for healing, but also in those who preach, teach or prophesy. As members of one Body, we have a serious responsibility to call believers to repent of their sin; we must not ignore their sinful lifestyles. It's rather amazing and ironic, but even when His children mess up, God seems to continue giving His gifts to us! He must really love us.

Some think no one is more gifted to heal in Jesus' Name than another. Yet certainly God gives different gifts to different members of the body of Christ! We each have different strengths and weaknesses and are called to a specific calling at which we should excel!

"But now God has placed the members, each one of them,
 in the body, <u>just as He desired</u>."
(1 Corinthians 12:18, emphasis mine)

"But one and the same Spirit works all these things,
 distributing to each one individually <u>just as He wills</u>."
(1 Corinthians 12:11, emphasis mine)

"All the members <u>do not</u> have the same function."
(Romans 12:4, emphasis mine)

Okay. So we are supposed to pray for the sick. I guess that makes sense, especially if I end up having the gift of healing! So how exactly would I go about "healing people"?

In the Bible, and perhaps you've already noticed, much of the time, those who ministered to the sick (both Jesus and the disciples) actually <u>commanded</u> that the illness leave, or that the person just stand and be healed. (For examples, see **John 5:3-9**; **Acts 3:6**; and **Acts 9:34**.) That requires a lot of boldness on the pray-er's behalf! And faith! Also important when praying for the sick, lame, deaf, blind or otherwise ill is to use Jesus' Name. We can read some of Jesus' teachings about this in the book of John:

"Whatever you ask in My name, that will I do, so that the Father may be glorified in the Son. If you ask Me anything in My name, I will do it."
(John 14:13-14)

"You did not choose Me but I chose you, and appointed you that you would go and bear fruit, and that your fruit would remain, so that whatever you ask of the Father in My name He may give to you."
(John 15:16)

"In that day you will not question Me about anything. Truly, truly, I say to you, if you ask the Father for anything in My name, He will give it to you."
(John 16:23)

In **Acts 3:6**, Peter obeys the Lord when he commanded the lame man to walk "In the name of Jesus Christ the Nazarene."

That's why we always finish our prayers, "In Jesus' Name!"

You got it! There is power in the Name of Jesus Christ.

It is Jesus who is actually healing, because:

> "for by His wounds you were healed."
> **(1 Peter 2:24)**

I should take some time to mention that it's not only important to pray for those <u>outside</u> of the Church for healing to preach the Gospel, but we are also told to pray for our sick brothers and sisters in the Church. James taught Christians how to go about praying for healing:

> "Is anyone among you sick? Then he must call for the <u>elders of the church</u> and they are to <u>pray over him, anointing him with oil in the name of the Lord</u>; and the <u>prayer offered in faith</u> will <u>restore the one who is sick</u>, and the Lord will raise him up, and if he has committed sins, they will be forgiven him. Therefore, confess your sins to one another, and <u>pray for one another so that you may be healed</u>. The effective prayer of a righteous man can accomplish much."
> **(James 5:14-16**, emphasis mine)

You can see that there are different methods for different circumstances. Only one of the examples that we have from the disciples or Jesus included anointing oil—**Mark 6:13**—but here in the book of James we are told to use it. Another interesting thing about this passage is that there seems to be a correlation between sickness and sin. The focus is on confessing our sins to make way for healing. Another passage that suggests sin is related to illness is found in **Psalm 32**:

> "When I kept silent about my sin, my body wasted away
> Through my groaning all day long.
> For day and night Your hand was heavy upon me;
> My vitality was drained away as with the fever heat of summer.
> Selah.

I acknowledged my sin to You,
And my iniquity I did not hide;
I said, "I will confess my transgressions to the LORD";
And You forgave the guilt of my sin. Selah." **(vv.3-5)**

The passage in **James** also commands us to confess our sins to one another. We know, because of **Romans 6:23**, that sin causes death in the world, so it makes sense that sin can also cause sickness. But, this does not mean that every illness is the result of sin. For example, in **John 9**, the disciples asked Jesus if a certain blind man was blind because of his parents' sin or because of his own. Jesus told them that his blindness was not as a result of sin:

"It was neither that this man sinned, nor his parents;
but it was so that the works of God might be displayed in him."
(John 9:3)

So we may never know why someone is sick or deaf or blind or whatever? Sometimes it may be caused by sin and sometimes it's not? That's a little confusing.

Sometimes if we ask, He will open our eyes and give us spiritual discernment and understanding. But our main focus should be to obey Him and pray for healing.

That takes a lot of faith, don't you think? I mean, I've known sick people that were prayed for, and they weren't healed. What do you say about that?

To that I say something that I heard a long time ago—trust God's Word, not your experience. It is difficult to understand and explain why God does not heal everyone, but it is something that happens. We have to trust Him. I do know that He still heals physical problems, and I also know that sometimes He chooses to heal the person in a different way. It really is up to Him!

I suppose that's good to know. But if I saw someone who was lame or deaf, well I don't think I have enough faith for those kinds of miracles!

That may be true, but the more you pray for healing, the easier it will be and the more faith and boldness you will have. Each time you obey the Lord, it becomes easier and easier. I guess the best way to learn how to pray for the sick is to be around people who already pray for healing so you can watch and learn from them. Like an apprentice!

But don't be afraid to try it by yourself. You can start with smaller sicknesses, like praying against headaches, or commanding fevers to leave in His Name. Or go straight for the big stuff! Ask the Lord for guidance, boldness and great faith. Then just go and do it!

> *The gift of healing is for building up the church and to further God's Kingdom on the Earth.*

HOW & WHY TO PRAY IN TONGUES

Praying in tongues is our next lesson.

What's 'praying in tongues'? What does that mean?

I'd like to introduce you to this exciting phenomenon called "the gift of tongues," also known as "a prayer language."

Speaking in tongues is probably the most mysterious gift that God gives His people. Before I go into more detail, let me say this. Praying in tongues consists of a person praying or speaking a language they have not previously studied or learned. This language may be a human language or an angelic language, as Paul pointed out in **1 Corinthians 13:1**.

So 'tongues' means 'language'?

Basically, yes! In the Bible, the gift of "tongues" is found throughout the book of Acts. In fact, Paul specifically instructed the early Church about this gift in his first letter to the Corinthians.

When Jesus told the twelve disciples that He would be leaving, He made it clear that it was best for Him to leave so the Holy Spirit (the "Helper") could be with them instead **(John 14:16; 16:7)**.

Prior to His ascension, Jesus said:

"You will be baptized with the Holy Spirit not many days from now... you will receive power when the Holy Spirit has come upon you; and you shall be My witnesses, both in Jerusalem, and in all Judea and Samaria, and even to the remotest parts of the earth" **(Acts 1:5,8)**.

Jesus also told the disciples to wait in Jerusalem until they received the baptism of the promised Holy Spirit **(Acts 1:4)**. Remember, the disciples had all previously been baptized with water. This baptism of the Holy Spirit must have been something else.

But how would they recognize what they were waiting for?

Good question. They didn't know either. Jesus had given hints, like in **Mark 16:17-18**, when He told them they would be able to speak other languages, pick up snakes without being harmed and heal the sick. But they didn't know how or when these things would happen.

While they waited, the 120 members of the earliest Church (including men and women) continually devoted themselves to prayer **(Acts 1:14)**.

On the day of the Jewish festival Shavuot (also called Pentecost, a festival celebrated fifty days after Passover), the sound of a very loud rushing wind came into the midst of these believers. As they looked around, there were "tongues of fire" resting on each of them. The early Church was on fire: a Holy Fire. As the Holy Spirit filled each of them, they suddenly began to "speak with other tongues" **(Acts 2:4)**.

Because of this festival, there was a large crowd of people from many nations gathered outside. Each person in the crowd heard the 120 believers speaking in the language he or she understood **(Acts 2:6)**! Instead of hearing Greek, the crowd heard about the "mighty deeds of God" in their native languages **(Acts 2:11)**.

Oh...so that's what speaking in tongues is? They knew other languages and people from all over the world could understand them?

That's part of it. This is the first biblical account of praying in tongues. The funny thing was that the crowd thought these people were drunk with wine! But that's just it. They didn't need wine—they had the Holy Spirit!

Whoa, whoa. Why did the crowds think they were drunk?

They must have sounded and looked pretty strange—that's probably why the crowds assumed they were drunk even though it was only 9 AM! They experienced tongues of fire, supernatural sounds, and speaking other languages—that was some pretty strange stuff, don't you think? Perhaps we would have accused them of being drunk too. This was the promised Holy Spirit baptism. Jesus told the Church to wait until they received the promised Holy Spirit, and this was quite an entrance! So do you think they recognized Him in all this fanfare?

Yeah!

God got the crowd's attention because He literally spoke their language! As the Church was busy proclaiming the wonderful works of God to the crowds present, Peter stood up and delivered the sermon that brought the first 3,000 people into the Kingdom of God **(Acts 2:41)**! Pretty incredible, right?

So there's your first lesson in the gift of tongues. It is a sign of the Holy Spirit and specifically, a sign to unbelievers. As Paul taught:

"So then tongues are for a sign, not to those who believe but to unbelievers" **(1 Corinthians 14:22)**.

Okay. Was praying in tongues only for people in the early Church? Like, when no one knew about Jesus?

No, the gift of tongues is for all believers, not only the early Church. We can see in Scripture that God doesn't take back His gifts. (See **Romans 11:29**.) The gift of tongues has an important purpose for the Church no matter what century we are living in. God gave this gift of speaking in tongues to strengthen the Church.

Besides, if you believe that God only gave gifts before the world knew about Jesus, consider this: there are still plenty of people in our world today who have never heard of Him either.

Alright, I think I get it. What kinds of people receive this gift? Do they have to be well-known? Is there an age requirement? Does it matter if they are male or female?

Peter quoted the prophet Joel, "I will pour forth of My Spirit on all mankind; and your sons and your daughters shall prophesy" **(Acts 2:17)**.

Like it is written in Galatians, "There is neither Jew nor Greek...neither male nor female; for you are all one in Christ Jesus" **(Galatians 3:28)**. Earthly fame does not influence decisions made by the King of Kings. Concerning age, I know at least two people who received their 'prayer language' at age 12! Age doesn't seem to be a factor, and neither is gender.

I've never heard anyone pray in tongues. What does it sound like?

It basically sounds like when you hear someone speak a language you don't understand. For example, if you heard someone speaking Estonian, it probably sounds like blabber to you, but the Estonians understand what they're saying. Here's the difference. Unless the Lord gives you an interpretation of the tongue you're speaking or there is an interpreter present, you won't understand what's coming out of your own mouth!

Weird. What's this about an interpreter?

That's another gift the Holy Spirit gives believers! It's mentioned in **1 Corinthians 12** and **14**, and it is pretty amazing. When someone who has the gift of interpretation hears another praying in tongues, he or she can understand what God is saying through them. Tongues can actually be a form of prophecy because God's voice is speaking through the person with the gift of tongues. The gift of interpretation is so important! It's really fun to see who God chooses to unite through the spiritual gifts—in order for the interpreter to use his or her gift, they must know someone with the gift of tongues!

God has important things to say through the gift of tongues. That's why it is also written: "Let one who speaks in a tongue pray that he may interpret" **(1 Corinthians 14:13)**. You should want to understand what you are saying.

That's pretty cool! You mentioned earlier that evangelism was not the only use for speaking in tongues. Before you tell me anything else, why would I want to "blabber"? Are there any benefits without an interpreter?

Besides speaking in a language that other people could possibly recognize, or that an interpreter could understand, praying in tongues is for YOU. It is your own prayer language. Paul wrote: "One who speaks in a tongue edifies himself" **(1 Corinthians 14:4)**.

Although your mind might not understand what your mouth is saying, praying in tongues makes your spirit stronger. Paul explained, "For if I pray in a tongue, my spirit prays, but my mind is unfruitful. What is the outcome then? I will pray with the spirit and I will pray with the mind also; I will sing with the spirit and I will sing with the mind also" **(1 Corinthians 14:14-15)**. "One who speaks in a tongue does not speak to men but to God; for no one understands, but in his spirit he speaks mysteries" **(1 Corinthians 14:2)**.

As you can see, it's important to pray with both the spirit AND with the mind.

Sweet! So, this is a gift that benefits me?

Yes! Exactly! But, like all of the spiritual gifts, praying in tongues also benefits the Church as a whole body **(1 Corinthians 14:26)**. I mentioned the gift of interpretation, and this gift is very useful for strengthening the Church. Someone prays in tongues, and another knows what God is speaking through that person. You see, when one person prays in tongues, he or she is letting God's voice speak through their mouth. In fact, Paul wrote, "If there is no interpreter, he (*the one who prays in tongues*) must keep silent in the church, and let him speak to himself and to God" **(1 Corinthians 14:28**, emphasis mine**)**. Paul taught the Romans, "The Spirit also helps our weakness; for we do not know how to pray as we should, but the Spirit Himself intercedes for us with groanings too deep for words" **(Romans 8:26)**. That is the gift of tongues in action! When you don't know what to say...pray in tongues! It is communion and fellowship with God the Holy Spirit that builds up your spirit and makes you stronger as a Christian!

Wow. It looks like this gift of tongues has a lot of benefits—both for me and for the Church in general. This is starting to look appealing...

Good! The Bible also says, "Desire earnestly spiritual gifts." (See **1 Corinthians 14:1**.) He must be tugging on your heart.

So, if I wanted to—ahem—'pray in tongues'...what would I do?

Just ask God! In the Bible, people received it in different ways. Sometimes, it's sudden and not requested **(Acts 2:2)**. Other times it was after someone laid hands on them **(Acts 19:6)**, and still others received it while they were listening to God's word being preached **(Acts 10:44-46)**. Sometimes the baptism of the Spirit preceded water baptism, and other times followed it. Of course you can always ask a fellow Christian to pray with you, too!

Wait, that's it? All I have to do is ask Him?

Well, before you do that, you must remember that God <u>wants</u> to give His children good gifts. He calls us His BELOVED. We are told to "pursue love, yet desire earnestly spiritual gifts" **(1 Corinthians 14:1)**. Of course, no one can predetermine what God will choose to do. Some people receive more gifts than others, and we each "have gifts that differ according to the grace given to us" **(Romans 12:6)**.

Well, what if I ask for this gift, but I don't receive it?

This is a valid question. Keep in mind, many people think that when they ask God for their own prayer language, it will feel magical, like POP ROCKS® in their mouth. Or you might expect your mouth to be forced open and your lips to mysteriously move without you controlling it. However, this is definitely not what typically happens! See, as with all the spiritual gifts, there is a certain amount of choice involved. For example, in order to prophesy, you must speak; you must pray for healing or the gift of healing will remain dormant, unused, unpracticed, and unseen.

So when you ask the Lord for the gift of tongues, immediately thank Him. Then open your mouth and start speaking. It is very difficult to explain the process, but like one of my friends has said, "Imagine you're jumping off a cliff and just go for it!" Some people receive many words (syllables) at once, others only a few. At first, many doubt that they actually received the gift. The key to growing in your prayer language is practice.

Hold up. I thought you said that you don't know what you are saying when you pray in tongues.

That's right. You don't know what you are saying, but you do have to practice. It can be kind of like learning English again. You will soon begin to recognize sounds and syllables. Sometimes, if you ask the Lord, He might tell you what you are saying.

I heard a story of a young man who only received one syllable that he knew to be tongues. Although he became discouraged, he repeated that one sound over and over for an entire year. One day as he prayed in his prayer language of one word, someone overheard him. She told him that it was the Hebrew word for "power!" He had actually prayed "power" over himself in the Holy Spirit for a whole year!

So, my friend, do not be discouraged if you feel, think, or say nothing that you consider special. Wait upon the Lord, and keep asking. Remember, you are His Beloved, and He is pleased when He looks at you.

If I do receive my own "prayer language," how should I use it in public?

That is a great question, and it's often disputed among believers. Some believe the gift of tongues should only be used when praying alone. Others believe you may pray in tongues both when alone and when praying with others. When you pray in tongues with others around, it is wise to speak quietly, almost under your breath. As the Scripture says:

> "But if there is no interpreter, he must keep silent in the church; and let him speak to himself and to God."
> **(1 Corinthians 14:28)**

If there is an interpreter nearby, make sure to stand next to them so they may understand and interpret so as to benefit the entire group. This next passage explains that when we come together, we are to use God's gifts appropriately and in turn.

> "What is the outcome then, brethren? When you assemble, each one has a psalm, has a teaching, has a revelation, <u>has a tongue</u>, <u>has an interpretation</u>. Let all things be done for edification. If anyone speaks in a tongue, it should be by two or at the most three, and each in turn, and <u>one must interpret</u>."
> **(1 Corinthians 14:26-27**, emphasis mine).

But I don't know anyone who can interpret tongues!

This is probably one of the reasons that the gift of tongues may not get much attention in the Church. It's a cycle: those with the gift of tongues don't want to disobey Scripture, so they are quiet because they are unaware of those who have the gift of interpretation. In the same way, those who have the gift of interpretation may not even know it because they have never heard anyone pray in tongues. They may wonder if anyone actually has the gift of tongues! Or, maybe they have only interpreted tongues once. When this happens, the gifts may not be used to their fullest potential, and this can prevent further unity within a Church body.

If you or anyone you know has the gift of tongues, remind them to pray for either an interpretation from God or an interpreter to come along! And if you know an interpreter, remind them to pray for something to interpret. The benefits of tongues and interpretation are amazing!

If I receive my own 'prayer language', how should I use it?

I have used it in many different circumstances. Have you ever been praying and you just felt far away from God? One solution is praying in tongues. As I mentioned before, using the gift of tongues strengthens your communion with God. It brings you closer to Him—remember, it is prayer! It's just not in your native language. You can also pray in English with your mind, but pray in tongues with your mouth at the same time, like Paul wrote:

> "For if I pray in a tongue, my spirit prays, but my mind is unfruitful. What is the outcome then? I will pray with the spirit <u>and</u> I will pray with the mind also." **(1 Corinthians 14:14-15**, emphasis mine).

I have also utilized the gift of tongues during worship. You can sing in tongues! Again, just like Paul wrote: "I will sing with the spirit and I will sing with the mind also" **(1 Corinthians 14:15)**. Singing in tongues is a lot of fun, and you can sing along with pre-written worship songs, just using your prayer language instead.

You said you can use it when you don't know what to pray, right?

Absolutely. Isn't the gift of tongues such a great gift from the Lord?

Yeah, maybe the best! Can one gift be better than another?

Well, don't go too far! Love is the very best gift from the Lord. "Love never fails; but if there are gifts of prophecy, they will be done away; if there are tongues, they will cease; if there is knowledge, it will be done away" **(1 Corinthians 13:8)**. None of the 'spiritual gifts' are as important as love.

And, let me show you **1 Corinthians 12:28**:

> "And God has appointed in the church, first apostles, second prophets, third teachers, then miracles, then gifts of healings, helps, administrations, various kinds of tongues."

I thought you said the gift of tongues is great. Why is it last in that list?

Being least in importance doesn't mean it's not a great gift! Remember that "every good thing given and every perfect gift is from above" **(James 1:17)**. God's gifts are perfect! It's just that some callings, like prophets and teachers, rank higher on the list of authority and importance in the Church body. It's obvious that healing and miracles are important in the Church, but not as important as the apostles or the prophets. Without the apostles, we wouldn't have churches, and without prophets we wouldn't even have the Bible! But without tongues, the Church could still survive. God gave it to us because it's still important, although not necessarily vital. Every gift has a place that God has given!

> "But one and the same Spirit works all these things, distributing to each one individually as He wills."
> **(1 Corinthians 12:11)**

I know you have said so much, but I have one more question. Why haven't I heard about this before? I've gone to church all my life, but I don't remember hearing about tongues.

One reason is what I mentioned earlier: the Bible instructs us not to pray loudly in tongues during church when there is no interpreter present. Finding an interpreter may not happen, so those with the gift of tongues just pray quietly so as to not be heard.

The other reason is what I mentioned at the beginning of this book: unbelief and confusion. It is easy to avoid a topic when it is widely misunderstood because of its potential danger. Yet, the Bible says, "Therefore, my brethren, desire earnestly to prophesy, and <u>do not forbid to speak in tongues</u>" (**1 Corinthians 14:39**, emphasis mine).

But don't let fear or confusion deter you from asking the Lord for the gift of tongues. It might seem weird at first, but the benefits make it worth asking Him for!

Praying in tongues is for building up the Church and to further God's Kingdom on the Earth.

HOW & WHY TO GIVE PROPHECY

Before you explain how and why to give prophecy, I want to know what prophecy is. Is it about the End Times? I remember prophecies about Jesus in the Old Testament, and I know there were prophets in the Old Testament, too. Is that the gift of prophecy?

Those are some great examples of biblical prophecy. But today, I would like to introduce you to the spiritual gift of prophecy. Jesus told us that we can hear His voice: "My sheep hear My voice, and I know them, and they follow Me" **(John 10:27)**. In its most basic form, the gift of prophecy involves one of God's children hearing a message from God and delivering it.

Are you telling me that Christians can hear God talk?

You betcha. And according to Scripture, prophecy is a pretty excellent gift from God! There were prophets in the Old Testament and in the New Testament too! Let's first look at the way Paul talks about the greatness of prophecy in **1 Corinthians** chapter **14** (emphasis mine):

- "Pursue love, yet desire earnestly spiritual gifts, but <u>especially that you may prophesy</u>." **(14:1)**
- "But <u>one who prophesies edifies the church</u>." **(14:4)**
- "Now I wish that you all spoke in tongues, but <u>even more that you would prophesy</u>" **(14:5)**
- "<u>greater is one who prophesies than one who speaks in tongues</u>" **(14:5)**

Paul says that prophecy is better than speaking in tongues? Why?

Well, we know it's not because he thinks tongues is good for nothing —he says, "I thank God, I speak in tongues more than you all" **(1 Corinthians 14:18)**. He teaches that prophecy is better because prophecy edifies the Church! Tongues do not instruct others, but prophecy does.

He said "one who prophesies edifies the church"? Huh?

All the spiritual gifts are for benefiting the Church, both individually and corporately. For example, without an interpreter, the gift of tongues is only for you. With an interpreter, it can be used to strengthen the members of the Church. But prophecy does not need an interpreter —prophecy can be a form of teaching.

Okay. I'm not sure I believe that people like me, in this day and age, can hear God talk. I need a few more concrete examples of prophecy before you go any further.

Sure. Let's start with the Old Testament. We know that God spoke to His people then, usually through a person who was known as a prophet. Moses, Samuel, Elijah, and Elisha were all prophets of God.

In **Numbers 12:6-8**, God told the people how He speaks to prophets.

> "He said, "Hear now My words: If there is a prophet among you, I, the LORD, shall make Myself known to him in a vision. I shall speak with him in a dream. Not so, with My servant Moses, He is faithful in all My household; with him I speak mouth to mouth, even openly, and not in dark sayings, and he beholds the form of the LORD."

God says He speaks to prophets in visions and dreams, but with Moses He actually spoke clearly. Other prophets include Ezekiel, Isaiah and Jeremiah—who could forget about their huge books in the Old Testament? Without a doubt, God spoke to them, and the Holy Spirit moved them to write it down for us. Technically, the entire Bible is prophecy because it's God speaking!

Wait. I thought prophecy was about telling the future.

Sometimes, yes. For example, many parts of the book of Revelation predict the future. But generally, the Hebrew understanding of prophecy was not only about the foretelling of events. Prophecy is God speaking to humans about what He plans to do or what He wants them to do, and it can involve the past, present or the future.

Okay, I'm glad I asked.

As I was saying, just look at the Bible. There was Jonah, Daniel, Micah, Amos, Hosea, Joel and various other people who were known as God's prophets. They authored books of the Bible and taught people to pay attention to God. Prophets also told the Israelites what they were doing well and what they were doing wrong. Sometimes, God even told these prophets how He was going to punish His people for their sin if they did not repent!

Can you share an example?

Well, let's look at King David. When David sinned with Bathsheba and had her husband killed, God used Nathan the prophet to show David his sin in **2 Samuel 12:1-15**. After explaining David's sin to him, Nathan spoke God's words:

> "Thus says the Lord, 'Behold, I will raise up evil against you from your own household…" **(2 Samuel 12:11)**

And when David did repent, Nathan gave him God's next message:

"The Lord also has taken away your sin; you shall not die. However, because by this deed you have given occasion to the enemies of the Lord to blaspheme, the child also that is born to you shall surely die." **(2 Samuel 12:13-14)**

That did indeed happen a few verses later. God used Nathan the prophet to point out sin in someone else's life **(v.1-10)**, to speak on behalf of God **(v.11)**, and to declare God's judgment on David for his sin **(v.13-14)**.

Speaking God's words must have been a big responsibility.

It still is. It's also a great honor. For another example, look at Jonah. The prophet Jonah was sent to Nineveh—(even though he didn't want to go)—and warned the kingdom that they would be overthrown in 40 days. As a result, everyone repented of their sin (see **Jonah 3:4-5**)!

He came to proclaim God's judgment and offer a chance for repentance—similar to what Nathan did for David. That's also what John the Baptist did in the New Testament, but we'll save that for later.

So, I have a question that may not have to do with prophecy. What exactly is repentance?

I'm glad you asked about this! Repentance is clearly important for anyone's relationship with God—otherwise these prophets wouldn't have spoken of it so many times!

Repentance is turning away from sin toward God. It involves choosing to obey God and turning away from sinfulness. The Greek word for repentance actually means "to change direction." When we repent, we choose to live for God instead of living for ourselves. Like **Romans 6:11** says, "Even so consider yourselves to be dead to sin, but alive to God in Christ Jesus." Saying "yes" to God means saying "no" to sin.

Thanks for explaining!

Isaiah is another great prophet of the Old Testament. His book is very large—God spoke a lot to him, including **Isaiah 53**—an entire prophetic chapter about Jesus Christ! He also spoke out against injustices toward the poor (for example, see **Isaiah 10:1-2**) and the Lord spoke through him to chastise the people for calling good evil, and evil good (**Isaiah 5:20**). Isaiah also gave an account of what many believe is heaven in **Isaiah 65**. Isaiah is an excellent book, and this prophet spoke God's words concerning lots of different things!

Sounds fascinating!

It is! There were also small groups of unnamed prophets that apparently traveled together. Here are two interesting examples:

- "When they came to the hill there, behold, <u>a group of prophets</u> met him; and the Spirit of God came upon him mightily, so that he <u>prophesied</u> among them." (**1 Samuel 10:10**, emphasis mine)

- "Then Saul sent messengers to take David, but when they saw <u>the company of the prophets prophesying</u>, with Samuel standing and presiding over them, the Spirit of God came upon the messengers of Saul; and <u>they also prophesied</u>. When it was told Saul, he sent other messengers, and <u>they also prophesied</u>. So Saul sent messengers again the third time, and <u>they also prophesied</u>. Then he himself went to Ramah and came as far as the large well that is in Sucu; and he asked and said, "Where are Samuel and David?" And someone said, "Behold they are at Naioth in Ramah." He proceeded there to Naioth in Ramah and the Spirit of God came upon him also so that he went along <u>prophesying</u> continually until he came to Naioth in Ramah." (**1 Samuel 19:20-23**, emphasis mine)

That seems both strange and intriguing. So people who weren't prophets could prophesy?

So it seems! And not only did prophets <u>speak</u> the words of God, but they were also prophetic signs to the people.

What does that mean?

Well, for example, God told Ezekiel to lie on his left side on the street for 390 days to represent 390 years that Israel sinned **(Ezekiel 4:4-5)**!

He stayed there for a year and a month?!

Uh-huh. Then the Lord told him to lie on his other side for 40 days to represent 40 years of sin that Judah committed **(Ezekiel 4:6-7)**. This, among other acts, was a sign to the people that God knew their sin.

Hosea was another prophetic sign to the people. In **Hosea 1:2**, God told Hosea to marry a prostitute to represent Israel's unfaithfulness to God. God often calls Himself a husband and His people His "Bride." Israel was a rather unfaithful bride—she always ran away from the Lord to worship other gods!

And Hosea represented God?

Yes, and his prostitute wife represented Israel. It's a beautiful picture of God's love and faithfulness toward His people, even when we aren't faithful toward Him.

> "If we are faithless, He remains faithful, for He cannot deny Himself." **(2 Timothy 2:13)**

I bet that sent a powerful message! Are there any more examples?

If you're willing to search for them in the Bible! But for now, let me show you some other interesting facts.

Before they were called 'prophets', they were known as 'seers' (see **1 Samuel 9:9**). They were called seers because they could *see* what many could not—spiritual things. Here are some examples.

- God showed Jeremiah images in his mind. These pictures are also known as visions. The pictures He showed him had prophetic meanings that God explained to him:

How & Why to Give Prophecy

"The word of the LORD came to me saying, 'What do you see, Jeremiah?' And I said, 'I see a rod of an almond tree.' Then the LORD said to me, 'You have seen well, for I am watching over My word to perform it.' The word of the LORD came to me a second time saying, 'What do you see?' And I said, 'I see a boiling pot, facing away from the north.' Then the LORD said to me, 'Out of the north the evil will break forth on all the inhabitants of the land.'"
(Jeremiah 1:11-14)

This is one way that God speaks to prophets—in pictures—remember that for later.

- Ezekiel and Isaiah both <u>saw</u> heaven
  (Ezekiel 1:22-28; Isaiah 6).

- In **2 Kings 6:17**, Elisha saw the armies of heaven and prayed that a certain servant would also see them! (He did!)

Thanks for all the Old Testament info. But you said the New Testament has prophecy too. Is that different from the Old Testament prophecy?

In **1 Corinthians 12:10** and **Romans 12:6**, prophecy is listed among the spiritual gifts. The New Testament is not particularly clear about <u>how</u> people prophesied, but we do have some examples of prophets and examples of prophecy in the Gospels **(Matthew, Mark, Luke & John)**:

- John the Baptist: He was a prophet—Jesus even made it clear in **Matthew 17:11-13** that John was the one that Malachi prophesied about—the Elijah to come in.

Wait. The Bible also says that John the Baptist wore camel's hair and ate locusts. Why should I pay attention to what he said?

Well, he was Jesus' cousin and he recognized Jesus as the Lamb of God who takes away the sin of the world **(John 1:29)**. His clothing was important because it was also reminiscent of what Elijah wore (see **1 Kings 1:8**). And just like many of the Old Testament prophets, John the Baptist preached a message of repentance:

> "Repent, for the kingdom of heaven is at hand."
> **(Matthew 3:2)**

And in **Matthew 4:17**, Jesus began His ministry on earth by preaching the same message:

> "From that time Jesus began to preach and say, 'Repent, for the kingdom of heaven is at hand.'"
> **(Matthew 4:17)**

Okay, if Jesus preached a similar message, I guess it's only right for me to give him some credit.

Here are some other examples of prophets and prophecy in the Gospels:

- **Luke 1:67** | "And his father Zacharias was filled with the Holy Spirit, and prophesied..." Zacharias prophesied about John the Baptist—his own son—in **Luke 1:68-79**.

- **Luke 2:36** | "There was a prophetess, Anna, the daughter of Phanuel, of the tribe of Asher."

- **John 11:49-52** | "But one of them, Caiaphas, who was high priest that year, said to them, 'You know nothing at all, nor do you take into account that it is expedient for you that one man die for the people, and the whole nation not perish.' Now he did not say this on his own initiative, but being high priest that year, he prophesied that Jesus

> was going to die for the nation, and not for the nation only, but in order that He might also gather together into one the children of God who are scattered abroad."

I see you using the words 'prophet', 'prophetess' and 'prophecy'. Is there a difference between a prophet and a person who prophesies?

Yes, I do believe there is. A 'prophet' is someone with great authority, who hears from God regularly and is well-trusted—he or she has a great track record with giving prophecy. I don't know many people who can officially be called 'prophets' today. When Paul explains the ranks within the Church offices, this is what he says:

> "And God has appointed in the church, first apostles, second prophets, third teachers, then miracles, then gifts of healings, helps, administrations, various kinds of tongues."
> **(1 Corinthians 12:28)**

So prophets hold an office in the Church, like an apostle or a teacher. It's more of a title, but giving prophecy is something that a normal, everyday believer might do.

And in Acts, we have a few more examples of prophets and prophecy.

Really? This is more prominent than I thought.

God's Word is full of this stuff! And I'm not even giving you most of it! Once you start looking, suddenly you will find it everywhere! Here we go:

PROPHETS AND PROPHECY IN ACTS (emphasis mine):

- **Acts 11:27-28** | "Now at this time some <u>prophets</u> came down from Jerusalem to Antioch. One of them named Agabus stood up and began to indicate by the Spirit that there would certainly be a great famine all over the world." One of the prophets present predicted a famine.

- **Acts 13:1** | "Now there were at Antioch, in the Church that was there, <u>prophets</u> and teachers…" The Church in Antioch (the first place the title 'Christians' was used) had prophets.

- **Acts 15:32** | "Judas and Silas, also <u>being prophets themselves</u>, encouraged and strengthened the brethren with a lengthy message." These missionary prophets encouraged the Christians at Antioch.

- **Acts 19:5-6** | "When they heard this, they were baptized in the name of the Lord Jesus. And when Paul had laid his hands upon them, the Holy Spirit came on them and they began speaking with tongues and <u>prophesying</u>." After they were baptized, these believers spoke in tongues and <u>prophesied</u>.

Alright, I'm convinced. Prophecy exists. It's a spiritual gift, and God has always spoken to His people. But why is prophecy important today? What does it do for me? Isn't the Bible enough prophecy on its own?

Let me answer your question with another question. Why wouldn't prophecy be important? You said that you've heard very little about prophecy besides end-time prophecy and foretelling about Jesus in the Old Testament. You now know that prophecy is all throughout the Bible—in the Old Testament and the New. I explained earlier that prophecy is not always about the future. Paul encouraged believers in the Corinthian Church to desire to prophesy, because "one who prophesies speaks to men for <u>edification</u> and <u>exhortation</u> and <u>consolation</u>" (**1 Corinthians 14:3**, emphasis mine).

What are 'edification' and 'exhortation' and 'consolation'? Are these necessary in my relationship with God?

Any individual prophecy may actually include all three of these things. I'll try to break it down for you, and then you can decide for yourself if prophecy might be beneficial for your relationship with the Lord.

First, prophecy is for edification. Edification gives empowerment, encouragement and strength. A young Christian (or a Christian feeling weak or faithless) can be edified—strengthened—by a prophetic word!

AN EDIFYING PROPHETIC WORD CAN BE USED TO:

- Confirm that you are on the right path
- Confirm that you have heard God's voice on your own
- Speak to your heart and increase your confidence about yourself as a person

One of the very first prophecies I received was an edifying prophecy. I was told, "He sees your praise, and is well-pleased." This brought joy to my heart and strengthened my confidence—God saw my praise! When I was feeling led to change my major in college, God used a few prophetic words to encourage me, in effect, saying, "Yes, you're following the path I have for you! Don't worry!" This type of prophecy is especially encouraging when you're not sure if you're hearing God's voice on your own.

Remember what we read earlier—the prophetic missionaries "encouraged and strengthened the brethren." That's what prophecy does!

This kind of prophecy does seem important! It reminds me of when I want affirmation. If someone else tells me I'm doing well, I feel good about myself.

I also feel a lot of joy when I receive an edifying prophecy.

Okay, I understand edification more now. What's next?

Prophecy is for exhortation. Exhortation is a challenge that may encourage one to meet a godly standard, help them have a new perspective on an old problem, encourage them to look forward to the future, or assist them in growing stronger.

Are you saying that a prophecy could help me when I feel too exhausted to serve God?

That's exactly right. In fact, there is a perfect scriptural example of exhortation in **Galatians 6:9**:

> "So let's not get tired of doing what is good. At just the right time we will reap a harvest of blessing if we don't give up" (NLT).

Prophecies that 'exhort' can motivate and uplift the receiver.

I like that example. I would probably feel refreshed and better able to serve God after hearing encouragement.

Proverbs 29:18 says, "Where there is no vision, the people perish" (KJV). Our God knows that we must have motivation to push us along. For this reason, He graciously exhorts us with prophecy, raising the bar so that we have something to achieve.

Timothy apparently needed some good exhortation. Paul told him, "Do not neglect the spiritual gift within you" **(1 Timothy 4:14)**. And, (this is one of my favorites!) Paul also told Timothy:

> "This command I entrust to you, Timothy, my son, in <u>accordance with the prophecies</u> previously made concerning you, that <u>by them you fight</u> the good fight, keeping faith and a good conscience." **(1 Timothy 1:18-19**, emphasis mine)

Paul actually commanded Timothy to remember the prophecies he received because the prophetic words would help him fight well as a Christian! Exhortation does that—it helps us fight with more passion and courage!

I have an excellent example from my own life of exhortation. I received ten prophecies from different people—and they all told me the same thing! God knows me well enough to know that one time was simply not enough. I needed a lot more encouragement to really get me moving! He used all of those people to give me prophetic words that would inspire and encourage me to work harder at a goal that He set for me.

Ten different times? Now I'm curious. Did you do something wrong to hear from God that many times?

No, but it's funny you should bring that up. A prophecy full of exhortation can also come through a correction. The Bible teaches us to "admonish the unruly" **(1 Thessalonians 5:14)** and, "If your brother sins, go and show him his fault in private" **(Matthew 18:15)**. If God ever reveals to you a sin that has been committed, before confronting the one who sinned, consider how to present your knowledge as an exhortation. For example, instead of saying, "You have been sexually immoral! You must repent!" you might say, "I believe the Lord is requiring purity from you: purity of mind, body and spirit. Listen to Him and obey His voice. Do not turn toward evil, but look to Him."

But if God showed me that my friend was sinning, why shouldn't I just tell him or her?

Simply, we must always be "speaking the truth in love" **(Ephesians 4:15)**. The spiritual gifts cannot be used correctly without the fruit of the Spirit: love, joy, peace, patience, kindness, gentleness, goodness and self-control **(Galatians 5:22-23)**. Jesus said we would distinguish the sheep from the wolves by judging their fruit **(Matthew 7:15-19)**. In other words, the fruits of the Spirit reflect our relationship with God—if you don't exhibit those fruits, you are in no better shape than the one whose sin you are correcting!

So you're saying, even if I know their sin, I still need to be kind and gentle?

Yes! The Bible says, "The kindness of God leads you to repentance" **(Romans 2:4)**. But that doesn't mean God won't use a prophecy to warn you to stop sinning. "He disciplines us for our good, so that we may share His holiness" **(Hebrews 12:10)**.

What if I actually see my friend sinning, can I confront him or her and point out the sin?

Absolutely. Like I mentioned before, **Matthew 18** is clear that we have a responsibility toward our brothers and sisters in the Lord. There is a difference between God telling you something and you witnessing it. If He reveals your brother or sister's sin, you might not have the whole picture and He may just want you to pray. But if you actually witness sin being committed, it is definitely your responsibility to confront your friend in grace, love, and truth.

So what is prophecy for?

Exhortation, edification and consolation! Edification encourages, and exhortation corrects and motivates. And what is consolation?

I like to describe consolation as comfort with hope. Jesus is called the "Wonderful Counselor" in **Isaiah 9:6**. Giving consolation is important because of our deep need to be loved, comforted, and filled with hope in times of despair. God cries with us when we cry, just like we are commanded in **Romans 12:15**—"Rejoice with those who rejoice, and weep with those who weep." When Jesus was preparing His disciples for His death, He said, "I will not leave you as orphans; I will come to you" **(John 14:18)**. Jesus saw that they were sad, and spoke to them concerning the future:

> "But because I have said these things to you, sorrow has filled your heart. But I tell you the truth, it is to your advantage that I go away; for if I do not go away, the Helper will not come to you; but if I go, I will send Him to you." **(John 16:6-7)**

The best consolation gives hope in the midst of fear or despair, and it lifts our head to look forward to better times when the distress is over.

It looks like prophecy is really all about God knowing us.

Yes! That's why it's so wonderful! God knows what we need to hear, whether it is edification, exhortation or consolation, and He will provide all our needs in Christ Jesus **(Philippians 4:19)**. God is "intimately acquainted with all my ways" **(Psalm 139:3)**. The Bible says, "You know when I sit down or stand up. You know my thoughts even when I'm far away **(Psalm 139:2 NLT)**.

So now what do you think of the gift of prophecy? What's your conclusion—important or not?

I'm really surprised! Prophecy actually does seem both important and helpful for my relationship with God!

I'm so glad you think so! Let's look at another verse explaining the role of prophecy in the Church.

Okay! I feel like I've only heard the beginning!

You have!

> "Prophecy is for a <u>sign</u>, not to unbelievers but to those who believe." (**1 Corinthians 14:22**, emphasis mine)

Prophecy is a <u>sign</u> to believers.

Prophecy is a sign? But why do I need a sign? I already believe in Him!

While the Scriptures are not entirely clear on why believers need a sign, here are some reasonable explanations:

- "<u>Signs</u>" can be proof of God's love and existence that we can remember and cling to when we're doubtful. Remember Thomas said he wouldn't believe Jesus was raised from the dead unless he put his finger in His wounds **(John 20:24-29)**? Most of us, if we're honest with ourselves, have been through times when we've questioned whether or not God is real.

Yeah, I can see that.

How & Why to Give Prophecy

- "Signs" from the Lord can show us how intimate He is with us—that we who love God are truly "known by Him" **(1 Corinthians 8:3)**. Like the verses I showed you earlier from **Psalm 139**, God really "searches the hearts" **(Romans 8:27)** and knows your thoughts **(1 Corinthians 2:11)**. Only God knows your pain, your joy and your anxieties. A prophecy may be the perfect 'sign' that shows you how well God knows you!

- "Signs" give direction. Like a lost driver who sees a street sign pointing him or her in the direction he or she wants to go, a prophecy can bring peace to replace confusion and fear of the future. How many times have you heard the phrase, "I need a sign!?" We are told that God has prepared things for us to do **(Ephesians 2:10)**, and Paul prayed that we will know God's will **(Colossians 1:9)**. You can also read in **Romans 12:4** that in the family of God, "all the members do not have the same function." It's okay, and even important to ask God about His plan for us—whether it's for your personal life, your future, or for the world. Prophecy can be the sign you're looking for. **Deuteronomy 19:15** says, "On the evidence of two or three witnesses a matter shall be confirmed"—He encourages us to ask for confirmation when we're not sure.

Okay. Prophecy is for a sign.

And edification, exhortation and consolation!

Now that I know better what prophesy is, who can do it? Are there special qualifications?

Let's look at Scripture. In **Acts 2**, Peter spoke and quoted the prophet Joel:

> "Your sons and your daughters shall prophesy...even on my bond slaves, both men and women, I will in those days pour forth of My Spirit and they shall prophesy." **(Acts 2:17, 18)**

So both men and women can prophesy?

You got it. And here's an example in Acts of female prophets:

> "On the next day we left and came to Caesarea, and entering the house of Philip the evangelist, who was one of the seven, we stayed with him. Now this man had <u>four virgin daughters who were prophetesses</u>." **(Acts 21:8-9**, emphasis mine)

God says men and women can prophesy. What about me? Can I prophesy?

Sounds exciting, doesn't it? (It is!) Now, I can't speak for God on this, because remember, "We have gifts that differ according to the grace given to each of us" **(Romans 12:6)**. God only knows if you will receive the gift of prophecy. But at least you're obeying the word that I mentioned at the beginning of this conversation: "Pursue love, yet desire earnestly spiritual gifts, but <u>especially that you may prophesy</u>." **(1 Corinthians 14:1**, emphasis mine). You <u>should</u> want to prophesy!

Now how about false prophets?

Excellent question. I like to know what you're really thinking when I'm teaching you. To be sure, false prophets do exist. Let's explore some different areas in the Bible when false prophets are mentioned. What verse do you think of when you think of false prophets?

I think there's a passage in Deuteronomy about false prophets, right?

Correct. Let's look at it together.

> "But the prophet who speaks a word presumptuously in My name which I have not commanded him to speak, or which he speaks in the name of other gods, that prophet <u>shall</u> <u>die</u>. You may say in your heart, 'How will we know the word which the LORD has not spoken?' <u>When a prophet speaks in the name of the LORD, if the thing does not come about or come true</u>, that is the thing which the LORD has not spoken. The prophet has spoken it presumptuously; <u>you shall not be afraid of him</u>."
> (**Deuteronomy 18:20-22**, emphasis mine)

Here we have the Lord God explaining what a false prophet is. He also instructs the people to not be afraid of a false prophet, saying, "That prophet shall die." Let's take a look at another group of verses, this time from **1 Chronicles**.

> "And it came about, when David dwelt in his house, that David said to Nathan the prophet, 'Behold, I am dwelling in a house of cedar, but the ark of the covenant of the LORD is under curtains.' Then Nathan said to David, 'Do all that is in your heart, for God is with you.' It came about the same night that the word of God came to Nathan, saying, "Go and tell David My servant, 'Thus says the LORD, "You shall <u>not</u> build a house for Me to dwell in…"
> (**1 Chronicles 17:1-4**, emphasis mine)

What do you see happening here?

Nathan spoke presumptuously! Does that mean he was a false prophet?

David greatly trusted Nathan. The Bible does not record that he was put to death; neither does it say that Nathan was speaking on behalf of other gods. He spoke presumptuously and assumed God would be okay with David building a temple for him. Surprisingly, God did not agree. Nathan went back to David the next day to tell him God's real answer (see **1 Chronicles 7:4-15**).

So you see, as in the example of Nathan, even some prophets in the Bible did not always speak perfectly. I'm not excusing false prophecies, but just like there is a difference between a prophet and prophecy, there appears to be a difference between false prophets and false prophecies.

Let's look closer at that last passage from Deuteronomy.

> "But the prophet who speaks a word presumptuously in My name which I have not commanded him to speak, or which he speaks in the name of other gods, that prophet shall die. You may say in your heart, 'How will we know the word which the LORD has not spoken?' When a prophet speaks in the name of the LORD, if the thing does not come about or come true, that is the thing which the LORD has not spoken. The prophet has spoken it presumptuously; you shall not be afraid of him."
> **(Deuteronomy 18:20-22)**

How does **Deuteronomy 18:20-22** define false prophets?

A false prophet is a person who speaks 'presumptuously' in God's Name.

Yes. So how do you know if someone is speaking presumptuously? Often times, you can't. This is why there are false teachers. It's not

How & Why to Give Prophecy

that the teacher is not really a teacher, but rather that he or she is teaching incorrect things. In the same way, the word 'false' in 'false prophet' means that he (or she) is not speaking the truth. In this passage, one way God says you can recognize a false prophet is by waiting to see if his word comes true. That could actually take a long time.

How else does God define a false prophet in that passage?

A person who speaks for other gods.

Sometimes people claim to be Christians, but they preach a different gospel. You must know the Scriptures to easily recognize this type of false prophet. Other religions have teachers who speak on behalf of "other gods," as in the passage from Deuteronomy. These are also considered false prophets, because they are not preaching the Gospel of Jesus Christ; they represent a false religion.

So false prophets are usually not true Christians?

Interesting way to put that. I would agree.

What did Jesus say about false prophets?

Great question. It's so important to understand what He said.

Just as Peter knew he was in the last days (see **Acts 2:14-17**), we also are in the end times. When Jesus talked of the end times, He notably said, "For false christs and false prophets will arise and will show great signs and wonders, so as to mislead, if possible, even the elect" **(Matthew 24:24)**. So, of course, we will see an abundance of false prophets. Jesus wanted us to recognize them.

Mark 13:22 also says that false prophets will arise and even show signs and wonders to lead people astray from the Lord. So a false prophet is not necessarily someone who has no power. False prophets can make miracles happen!

Wait! If they have power, how am I supposed to recognize a false prophet when compared to a true one?

In addition to what I showed you from **Deuteronomy**, the Lord Jesus teaches us another way to recognize false prophets. **Matthew 7:15-16** (emphasis mine) says, "Beware of the false prophets, who come to you in sheep's clothing, but <u>inwardly are ravenous wolves. You will know them by their fruits</u>. Grapes are not gathered from thorn bushes nor figs from thistles, are they?" The sign of a false prophet will be his fruit—does he or she lead you away from God to worship something or someone besides Jesus?

If you want to know whether or not someone is a false prophet, ask yourself these questions:

- Is he or she filled with the fruit of the Spirit?
- Does he or she lead you into a closer relationship with God?
- Does he or she preach according to the Scriptures?
- Is this person living with kindness and patience, speaking according to the Bible, and quick to repent of sin?

If you consistently answered no, that person may be a false prophet.

That's confusing. People can walk around anywhere giving 'prophecy', but if I don't know them, how can I tell if they are a false prophet or not? I don't feel equipped to distinguish between false and true prophets —it seems nearly impossible.

How & Why to Give Prophecy

Sadly, because of that, much of the Church has altogether turned away from prophecy today. Yet the Scripture says:

> "Do not quench the Spirit; <u>do not despise prophetic utterances. But examine everything carefully</u>; hold fast to that which is good; abstain from every form of evil" (**1 Thessalonians 5:19-22**, emphasis mine).

We should not allow fear and confusion to turn us away from spiritual gifts such as prophecy. Jesus said that His sheep would hear His voice, but "a stranger they simply will not follow, but will flee from him, because they do not know the voice of strangers" **(John 10:5)**.

The better you know God, His Word and His love, and the more time you spend with Him, the more you'll be able to figure out what is from God and what is from satan. I can't emphasize enough the importance of knowing Scripture. **Hebrews 5:14** says that practice will teach us to discern good and evil. I've heard it said that the best way to figure out which paper money is counterfeit is to be familiar enough with the real thing. This is also true of learning to distinguish between true and false prophecy.

I guess I should start exercising my senses to figure out good and evil!

Absolutely! But do not allow yourself to be consumed with worry over false prophets. As I said earlier, they will exist. Instead, seek out godly teachers and focus on knowing Jesus and the Bible.

Now you've shown me that men and women can prophesy, I think I might be able to do it too. But how do I begin?

Before you begin, remember that as a born again believer in Jesus Christ, God Himself lives within you! His Holy Spirit is inside you.

(See **Romans 8:9-11** & **1 Corinthians 12:3**.) Then, ask Him to speak to you about the person you're praying for!

You're telling me it's as simple as asking?

It's always that simple when you start! Spiritual gifts are just that—gifts! God wants you to hear His voice! He loves you! But, remember that God distributes each of His gifts individually <u>as He wills</u> (**1 Corinthians 12:11**, emphasis mine). Prophecy may not be a gift He has decided to give you, and that's okay! Yet I believe that when necessary, God will talk with whoever is ready to listen.

True. Let's say I do have the gift of prophecy. How do I know when God is talking to me?

Isn't that what everyone wants to know! Like you said before, you've got to spend a lot of time with Him! Read the Bible, pray. Bible, Bible, Bible! Know the Bible! I can't say it enough. Scripture and love are the most important things to have when trying to hear from God. If you think you may have heard from God but what you 'heard' goes against what the Bible teaches, then you know that is not God talking. For example, if you 'hear' that it's okay to steal or cheat on a test, it's safe to say that you're not hearing from God. If you 'hear' that you are worthless, that is not God's voice! You are either hearing yourself or the enemy.

What if someone walks up to me and tells me something and they say it's from God, but I'm not so sure. What do I do then?

God does state in the Bible that it's important to ask Him to prove that the word is His. He also teaches through Paul's words: "Do not despise prophetic utterances. <u>But examine everything carefully, hold fast to that which is good</u>" (**1 Thessalonians 5:20-21**, emphasis mine).

It's very important to <u>examine</u> every prophetic word that you receive. Write them down, whether you receive many or just a few, and pray over them. Keep your prophecies close by so that you may fight the good fight of faith with them, like Paul instructed Timothy **(1 Timothy 1:18-19)**. Just like there are many ways to hear from God to prophesy, (as I will explain later), there are many ways that He can confirm that what you've heard is from Him. When someone gives you a prophecy (or, a "word from God," as they may say,) you can ask the Lord to prove that it was Him.

You can say something like, "Lord, is that true? Please give me confirmation." Then, He may give you a dream, or send other people to you to tell you the same thing! That's what happened to me—at least ten different people told me the same thing! That's how I knew it was really from God. And, as you learned, prophecy through another person can also be a confirmation. Like when I was in college and considering changing my major. Out of the blue, a stranger prayed for me and I received prophecy that confirmed I was also hearing God on my own! Getting confirmation can be more exciting than a prophecy! **2 Corinthians 13:1** explains that every word from God should have two or three confirmations.

Have you ever gotten goose bumps or had an experience where you felt God speaking to you?

I think so. Maybe.

Let's say that you have. A wonderful teacher I know labels this moment as "quickening." To "quicken" means "to give life to."* When God quickens something for us, He brings it life that we may recognize it is from Him. The Lord speaks through quickening all the time! This often comes through something we may refer to as a "coincidence."

---

* Sandy Warner, www.thequickenedword.com

Quickening brings life to normal words. But these moments are not coincidences; they come from the Lord and speak directly to you concerning a circumstance you are in the middle of. It's important to learn to recognize these moments, and pay special attention to them.

Is this something you learn with time?

Oh, yes! You can expect to have lots of what I would call practice. You may not be able to discern between God's voice and other influences right away, but as you continue to exercise the gift and even make mistakes, you will begin to understand how He speaks.

That makes sense. Hmm. I really should start reading the Bible more to find out how God speaks and how prophets heard Him.

You said it! God speaks in a multitude of ways. One of the ways I best recognize Him is when I get an answer before I finish asking Him my question! **Isaiah 65:24** says, "It will also come to pass that before they call, I will answer..."

God can also give you an image in your mind—this is called your "mind's eye." A biblical example of this is what Jeremiah saw. God may speak to you by showing you a single image—a vision. Let's say, for example, you might see a sheep. It could also be a moving picture, like a sheep eating grass. That is also a vision.

If God showed me these things, I would have no idea what He was saying!

This is another reason why knowing the Bible is so important! When you first see an image, you might immediately have understanding. Always pray and ask God what it means. Also, what you see may have a significant meaning in Scripture.

How & Why to Give Prophecy

Oh yeah! We are "the sheep of His pasture," or something like that?

That's **Psalm 100:3**! So, if you were praying for someone, and you saw a sheep in your mind, what might you tell the person?

That he or she is a child of God and God says so?

That's a great start. You're using the Bible to prophesy according to what God showed you. Make sure you ask God, because He may give you another understanding different from your own.

Another way God speaks to us about someone else is by reminding us of a Scripture. For example, the Lord may remind you of **Psalm 94:14**, "For the LORD will not abandon His people, nor will He forsake His inheritance." To give this as a prophecy, you could summarize it by saying: "God wants you to know He will not leave or abandon you," or you could just be straight-forward: "Read **Psalm 94:14**."
It is important to use Scripture while prophesying. Actually, it's a good idea to ask God for a Scripture every time you prophesy. Scripture is an anchor that holds us firmly in place and eliminates confusion.

Again with the Scripture! I see why it's so important. Does He speak in any other ways?

You may also have a feeling, or an impression about someone. When you ask the Lord what He wants to say, you might receive a vision or Scripture that completes the feeling. You may then choose to tell the person. Sometimes, images and visions might mean nothing at all. But take notice, just in case God is speaking!

God also gives answers to prayer and solutions to problems in so many other ways! You may read a book or an email, have a dream or a conversation, watch a movie or read the Bible, when suddenly you realize the solution. You could even glance at a billboard and recognize that it's God speaking in that moment! It's so much fun to listen for God; the key is to pay attention.

Phew! Does God ever speak in plain words or sentences? This all sounds like a puzzle!

Well, He does love puzzles and mysteries! Even Jesus' disciples got tired of hearing Him speak in parables. In **John 16:29** the disciples rejoiced when Jesus spoke 'plainly'—"At last You are speaking plainly and not figuratively" (NLT). But yes, He also speaks in sentences and words. I've heard Him in that way a few times, and it's so powerful!

Okay. So picture this. I'm praying for someone and then I see something ridiculous, like a ham and cheese sandwich!?

It's true that our minds can get in the way of actually hearing God's voice, but who knows—the person you are praying for may have a special memory connected with ham and cheese sandwiches and sharing this picture would reveal how intimate God is with him or her. You just have to ask that person! Otherwise you'll never learn the difference between your thoughts and His. You must test whatever prophecy you think you have received from God for another person. Our senses must be trained with practice (**Hebrews 5:14**).

Before you tell someone what you believe you heard from God, it's so important, especially when you first start, to begin with, "I believe the Lord is saying…" Be very humble about prophesying. Giving prophecy is a learning process. Even when you think you've mastered it, you can still fail. In fact, that moment when you think you know everything is a dangerous time.

> "Therefore let him who thinks he stands take heed that he does not fall." (1 Corinthians 10:12)

Ask the Lord for humility. And remember, prophecy is a gift. Don't take it for granted.

> "But one and the same Spirit works all these things, distributing to each one individually just <u>as He wills</u>."
> **(1 Corinthians 12:11**, emphasis mine)

After hearing all of this, I guess this spiritual gift can be both exciting and complicated! If I even want to think about prophesying, I really need to spend more time with God!

I'm glad you're honest enough to admit that. When people are deceived and confused, it's likely because they do not know the Bible well enough. Don't let that be you! Start reading, because God's Word is truth **(John 17:17)**!

But don't assume you need to wait until you have memorized the Bible. You can start asking Him for prophecy about others right now! Don't be afraid to start praying and asking God about people. Ask your friends for their prayer requests, and start praying. You will be amazed at what God does. And when someone else gives you a prophecy, remember what I told you earlier: ask God to confirm it through someone or something else. Don't forget to enjoy it! This is the beauty of the Body of Christ—we can speak to one another for the "edification and exhortation and consolation" of each member!
(1 Corinthians 14:3, 5).

How do I know if I heard incorrectly?

Before I share with someone what I believe the Lord wants them to know, I make it clear that I am still learning to hear God. I ask them if they have any response or if they can confirm what I told them. I open the door and invite them to respond, whether positively or negatively. It's so important to be humble and willing to receive correction.

What if I do get it wrong?

First, don't be discouraged. We've already spoken about practice. Keep trying! "For God has not given us a spirit of timidity, but of power and love and discipline" **(2 Timothy 1:7)**. Even if you hear incorrectly, don't be afraid to try again. People may not be healed every time you pray for healing, and you may not hear God every time you ask. But keep seeking, keep knocking, and you shall find. (See **Luke 11:9-10** AMP.) When He does answer, you won't forget it!

> *The gift of prophecy is for building up the church and to further God's Kingdom on the Earth before Jesus' second coming.*

CONCLUSION

As much as we can enjoy the spiritual gifts, there is at least one thing higher and more important than any of them.

> "Love never fails; but if there are gifts of prophecy, they will be done away; if there are tongues, they will cease; if there is knowledge, it will be done away" **(1 Corinthians 13:8)**.

Healing, tongues, prophecy, and knowledge are all inferior to **love**. When someone asked Jesus what the most important commandment was, this was His response:

> Jesus answered, "The foremost is, 'Hear, O Israel! The Lord our God is one Lord; and you shall <u>love</u> the Lord your God with all your heart, and with all your soul, and with all your mind, and with

all your strength.' The second is this, 'You shall <u>love</u> your neighbor as yourself.' There is no other commandment greater than these" (**Mark 12:29-31**, emphasis mine).

Jesus did not say that the most important command is to practice spiritual gifts. Instead, He taught that loving God is the most important commandment. Spiritual gifts didn't even place second in the list of important commandments! God's top priorities are that you love Him, and then you love others. It's really so simple.

> "But seek first His kingdom and His righteousness, and all these things will be added to you" **(Matthew 6:33)**.

It's easy to get carried away with spiritual gifts and lose focus on what is really important. Trust me—I've been there! The Bible does say, "Desire earnestly spiritual gifts," but there are far more verses commanding believers to desire the Lord. For example, here are some verses from Deuteronomy, 1 Chronicles and the Psalms.

> "But from there you will seek the LORD your God, and you will find Him if you search after Him with all your heart and with all your soul." **(Deuteronomy 4:29)**

> "Seek the LORD and His strength; seek His face continually!" **(1 Chronicles 16:11)**

> "And those who know Your name will put their trust in You, for You, O LORD, have not forsaken those who seek You" **(Psalm 9:10)**.

I also want to take a moment to exhort you. This book was written on the assumption that those who read it know Jesus Christ. If you know Jesus Christ as your Lord and Savior, you are a beloved child of God.

Having any one of these spiritual gifts we have studied together does not compare to the glory of knowing Christ Jesus!

But if you picked up this book without knowing the Lord Jesus, I do hope that you have now become curious about God!

So let me introduce you to the truth about Jesus Christ.

- He is God, who came to earth as a human to share in our sufferings and temptations.
- He is real and compassionate.
- Because He was a human, Jesus knows what it's like to be in pain.
- He even is willing to bear your pain and burdens.
- He is love.
- He is alive today.

The Bible explains that all humans are sinners.
Before you point out that you aren't a bad person, here are some examples of sin:

- lying
- stealing
- hatred
- murder
- fear
- anxiety/worry
- drunkenness
- lust
- sex outside marriage
- disrespecting parents or other authority figures
- gossip
- pride

Just to name a few! Looking at a list like that, who <u>hasn't</u> sinned? Certainly I have! And here's the effect that sin has on you.
(and everyone else):

DEATH

Yep. As even doctors have pointed out, fear, guilt, worry and anger have serious effects on our physical bodies—not to mention emotional effects or spiritual ones. Sin also separates you from God (see **Isaiah 59:4**). That's why when you pray, you might feel like God is ignoring you. You have actually separated yourself from Him because of the sin you've committed!

And there is another form of death too—eternal death in hell. Hell was made for satan and his demons—not for you—(see **Matthew 25:41**) but when sin is committed, there must also be punishment. For many, they will receive their punishment in hell. But there is hope.

Father God knew about the effects of sin. He made you so He could love you. He hates seeing you lost in sin and death, and He wants you to know the joy and love He offers to those who obey Him. So He chose to sacrifice His Son—Jesus Christ—in order to rescue you from this dead life and punishment in hell! Jesus came to earth, never sinned, sacrificed His body on a cross, died, and came back to life—He took the punishment that you deserved because of the sin you've committed in your past. Believe Him, turn away from your sin, and be refreshed by the God who loves you.

When you turn away from sin and towards Jesus Christ, ask His Holy Spirit to fill and baptize you. Then you will be dead to sin and alive to God through Christ Jesus your Lord (see **Romans 6:11**). Your next steps should include: reading the Bible, and looking for ways to please God. Ask God to guide you to a great church where you can learn and grow. Ask Him for the spiritual gifts, (listed in **1 Corinthians 12 & 14**, and **Romans 12**), and as you receive what He has planned for you, use it. Because when you receive any gifts from Him, God says that if you are faithful with a small amount, He knows you will be faithful in much. If you are faithful with little, He will be likely to trust you with more **(Matthew 25:23)**. So use whatever He gives you, no matter how big or small!

ACKNOWLEDGMENTS

Thank You, Holy Spirit, for challenging me to discover more about You and the gifts You have given to Your children! You lead me in paths of discovery. As You give to me, I will continue to share.

Thank you to all my friends & family who have enjoyed this journey of discovery with me, and to all of those who have shared insights from the Scriptures, including Sandy Warner, friends and mentors at both Messiah College, NewSong Community Church and St. Bartholomew's Anglican Church. May the Lord continue to reveal more to you.

Thanks to Kimberly Geshwein for allowing me the use of your fonts! They have added so much character to this book.

Thanks Keith (& Jenna!), for allowing me to share your quote.

Jamie, my sister in Christ. You've done a beautiful job designing this book! I am so blessed by your work, as well as your constant encouragement concerning my writing. Thank You for reminding me to use what I have written, and for handling all of my little requests very well! May you be blessed!

Rick, my husband, my love. Thank you for your excitement as I have embarked on this project. May the Lord continue to lead and bless us as we walk together "in this crazy life and through these crazy times." I love you!

If (and when!) the Lord gives you any of the spiritual gifts, remember to use them to bless and strengthen your brothers and sisters in Christ and to further God's Kingdom on the Earth before Jesus comes again!

Be faithful with all you receive!

Made in the USA
Middletown, DE
07 September 2015